Reading STREET

Grade K

Scott Foresman

Practice Book 5
Unit 5

PEARSON

Scott Foresman

Editorial Offices: Glenview, Illinois • Parsippany, New Jersey • New York, New York
Sales Offices: Needham, Massachusetts • Duluth, Georgia • Glenview, Illinois
Coppell, Texas • Sacramento, California • Mesa, Arizona

ISBN: 0-328-14513-0

23 V0B4 13

© Pearson Education K

Contents

Unit 5
Going Places

Circle the pictures that begin with /j/. Color the pictures that begin with /w/.

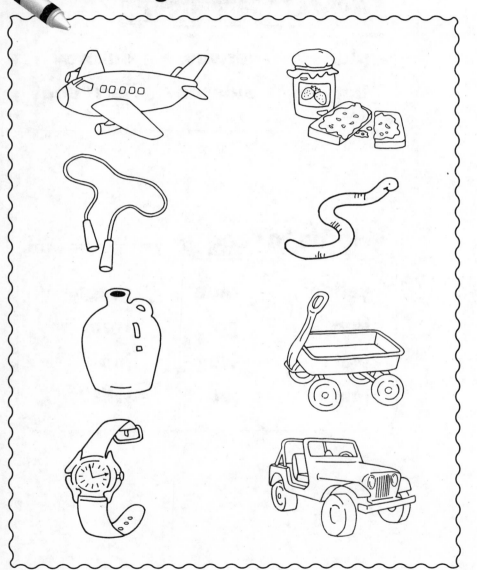

4

Family Times

You are your child's first teacher!

This week we're ...

> **Reading** *Max Takes the Train*

Talking About Ways to Travel

Learning About Connect /j/ to *Jj* and /w/ to *Ww*
Realism and Fantasy

1

Here are ways to help your child practice skills while having fun!

Day 1 **Read Together**

Write *j* or *w* on ten small cards. Mix the cards and place in a pile. Have your child take a card and say a word that begins with the letter on the card. For succeeding games, help your child write sentences for the words he or she names.

Day 2 **Read Together**

Have your child read the Phonics Story *Jen and Will*. Find words that have /j/ or /w/.

Day 3 **Connect /j/ to *Jj* and /w/ to *Ww***

Have your child add the letters *j* or *w* to make new words. Ask him or her to read each word.

_am   _ob   _ell   _in   _et   _ill

Day 4 **Questions**

Remind your child that questions are sentences that ask something. Say one of the following words and help your child make a question that starts with that word: *who, what, when, where, why, how, can, are, do, does*.

Day 5 **Practice Handwriting**

Have your child write the following question. Encourage him or her to create an answer to the question.

Will Jill jump and win?

Words to talk about

| plane | jetway | subway |
| tunnel | sidecar | ferryboat |

Words to read

yellow	blue	green
here	go	from
wet	wag	job
jam	jet	will

Name _____

 Write   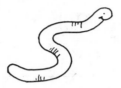 Color

Jj
Ww

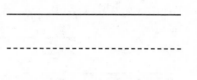

Directions: Name each picture. Write *j* if the word begins with /j/. Write *w* if the word begins with /w/. Color the /j/ pictures.

School + Home **Home Activity:** Have your child find other words with /j/ or /w/.

Practice Book Unit 5

Phonics Consonants *Jj*/j/, *Ww*/w/ **3**

Name _____

 Write  Color

| yellow blue green have |

_____

- - - - - - - - - - - - - - - -

The pond is _____ .

_____

- - - - - - - - - - - - - - - -

My top is _____ .

_____

- - - - - - - - - - - - - - - -

Is the sun _____ ?

_____

- - - - - - - - - - - - - - - -

I _____ a cat.

Directions: Read each sentence. Have children write the missing word to finish each sentence and color the pictures.

School + Home **Home Activity:** Have your child use the high-frequency words in other sentences.

You can get on the big, blue jet.

You can go with Jen and Will.

Phonics Story *Jen and Will*
Target Skill Consonants *Jj/j/, Ww/w/*

Jen and Will

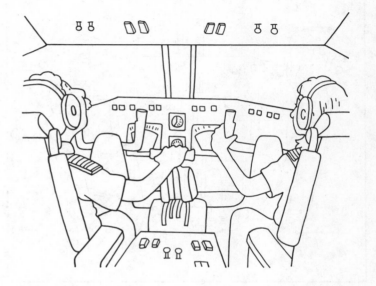

Jen and Will get on the jet.

It is a big, blue jet.

Jen and Will have jobs
on the jet.

Jen and Will like the job.

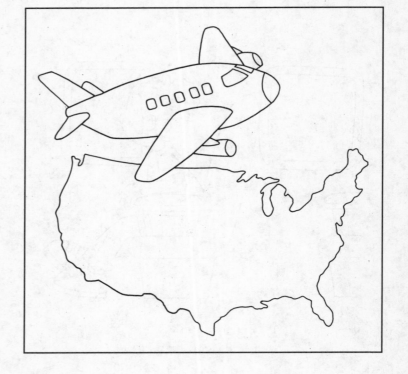

Jen and Will get the jet
to go.

They can see you.

Name _____

✏️ **Write**

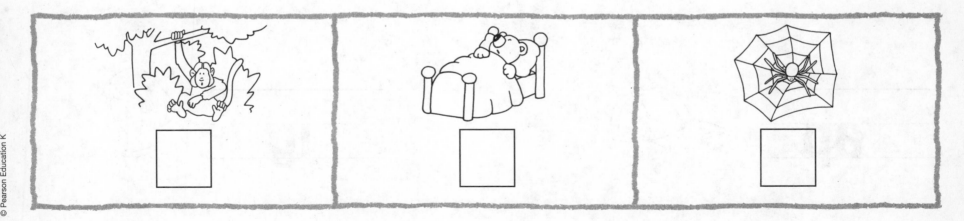

Directions: Label the animal in each picture *R* for real or *M* for make-believe.

 Home Activity: Draw and color a picture of a real animal and where it lives.

Comprehension Realism and Fantasy **7**

Name _____

 **Write**    **Color**

_____
et

_____
am

Jj

Ww

_____
eb

_____
ed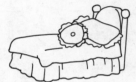

_____
ap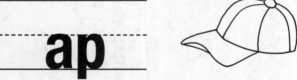

_____
ig

 Directions: Write *j* if the word begins with /j/. Write *w* if the word begins with /w/. Color the /j/ and /w/ words.

 Home Activity: Have your child draw pictures of things that begin with /j/ and /w/.

8 **Phonics** Consonants *Jj/j/, Ww/w/*

Practice Book Unit 5

Name _____

 Circle  Color

 Directions: Circle the make-believe pictures. Color the real pictures.

 Home Activity: With your child, look at a book about how real animals live.

Practice Book Unit 5

Comprehension Realism and Fantasy **9**

Name _____

 **Draw**

Can you jog?

I like to skip.

Do you like to skip?

I can jog.

Can you hop?

I can get the bell.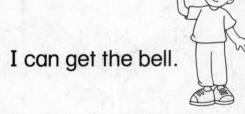

Can you get the bell?

I can not hop.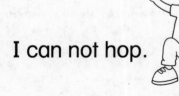

 Directions: Draw a line from each question to its answer.

School + Home **Home Activity:** Ask your child the questions and have him or her create an answer.

10 **Grammar** Questions

Color the pictures that end with /ks/.

Family Times

You are your child's first teacher!

This week we're ...

Reading *Mayday! Mayday!*

Talking About Emergency Transportation

Learning About Connect /ks/ to *Xx*
Cause and Effect

Here are ways to help your child practice skills while having fun!

Day 1

Read Together

Write one of these sentences on a sheet of paper: *I see an ox on a box. I can mix and fix it. I like Rex the fox.* Read a sentence together. Ask your child to circle the words that end with /ks/.

Day 2

Read Together

Have your child read the Phonics Story *Max*. Find words that have /ks/.

Day 3

Connect /ks/ to Xx

Say pairs of words and have your child tell which word ends with /ks/: *mix, mill; fit, fix; tap, tax; six, sit; fan, fax.*

Day 4

Question Marks and Uppercase Letters

Write these sentences on cards: *I am five. Am I five?* Have your child read each sentence and tell how they are alike and how they are different. Point out the uppercase letters and the period and question mark. Continue with: *I can run. Can I run?*

Day 5

Practice Handwriting

Have your child write the words. Then have him or her write several of the words using all capital letters.

fix   wax   Rex   fox   six   mix

Words to talk about

rescue	pilot	yacht
sailor	mechanic	shimmering

Words to read

yellow	blue	green
one	three	five
box	mix	wax
six	fix	fox

Name _____

 Circle  **Color**

dog

sat

_____

She _____ on the bus.

look

yet

_____

We _____ up at a jet.

hat

ran

_____

My dog _____ to me.

see

bag

_____

_____ my cat!

hop

leg

_____

He can _____.

bell

sit

_____

Can I _____ here?

 Directions: Circle the verb that matches the picture.
Write the word to complete the sentence.

 Home Activity: Have your child read each sentence.

60 **Grammar** Verbs

Practice Book Unit 5

Name _____

 Circle  Color

 Directions: Circle the picture in the third box to tell how Ann gets to school. Color the pictures. Circle the picture in the third box to tell which kitten Joe gets. Color the pictures.

 Home Activity: Have your child tell why he or she drew the conclusion he or she did.

Name_____

 Write  Color

_____
__ilt__

_____
__am__

_____
__ack__

Yy
Qq

_____
__ak__

_____
__ick__

_____
__ell__

© Pearson Education K

 Directions: Name each picture. Write *y* if the word begins with /y/. Write *qu* if the word begins with /kw/. Color the /y/ pictures.

 Home Activity: Have your child draw pictures of things that begin with /y/ and /kw/.

Name _____

 Write   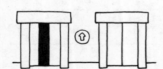 Color

Uu

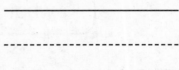

 Directions: Name each picture. Write *u* on the line if the word begins with /u/. Color the /u/ pictures.

 Home Activity: Look through a newspaper or book with your child and point out words that begin with /u/.

Name _____

 **Write**  **Color**

| what | was | said | she |

_____

_____ she with you?

_____

_____ is my mom.

_____

He _____ she was with me.

_____

_____ did you see?

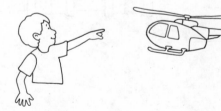

Directions: Have children write the missing word to complete each sentence. Color the pictures.

School + Home **Home Activity:** Have your child use the high-frequency words in other sentences.

24 **High-Frequency Words**

Practice Book Unit 5

Jud ran to his pals.

Jud said, "Let us go in!

We will have fun!"

4

Phonics Story *Fun for Jud*
Target Skill Short *Uu/u/*

Fun for Jud

The sun was hot.

Jud got up from bed.

1

Jud has to have a plan.

What can he do for fun?

Jud will see his pals.

What will they do for fun?

Name _____

✏️ Color

 Directions: Color each matching pair a different color.

School + Home **Home Activity:** Have your child compare and contrast the bike messengers by telling how the pictures are alike and how they are different.

Name _____

 Write  Color

_____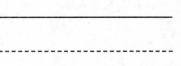

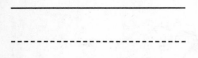

_____

_____

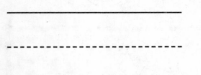  _____

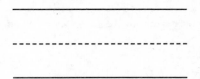 

_____

 _____

 Directions: Name each picture. Write the letter for the middle sound of each word. Color the /u/ pictures.

 Home Activity: Help your child make a list of words with /u/.

28 **Phonics** Short *Uu*/u/

Practice Book Unit 5

Name _____

 Color

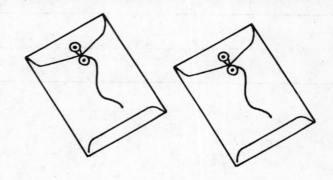

Directions: Color pairs of pictures that are alike.

 Home Activity: Have your child tell how the pairs of pictures are alike or different.

© Pearson Education K

Name _____

 Write  Draw

April 10, 2005

_____

- -

_____

_____

- -

_____

 Directions: Copy the date in the first box. Write today's date in the second box and draw a picture of something you did today.

 Home Activity: Have your child read the date and name the days of the week.

30 **Grammar** Dates

© Pearson Education K

Color the path of pictures with /u/.

4

Family Times

You are your child's first teacher!

This week we're ...

Reading *The Little Engine That Could*

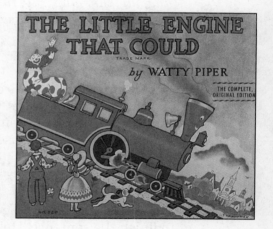

Talking About How Trains Move

Learning About Connect /u/ to *Uu*
Plot

1

Here are ways to help your child practice skills while having fun!

Read Together

Write the following words on a sheet of paper. Have your child read the /u/ words.

nut   gum   bug   pup

Read Together

Have your child read the Phonics Story *Jan and Gus.* Find /u/ words.

Connect /u/ to *Uu*

Write the word *bug* on a sheet of paper. Tell your child to change the first letter and make new words *(hug, jug, lug, mug, rug, tug).* Continue with the word *cub (hub, rub, tub, sub).*

Nouns

Have your child bring three of his or her favorite toys. Ask your child what the items are. Tell your child that he or she is using nouns to say the items. Then ask your child to use the words in sentences.

Practice Handwriting

Have your child write the sentence and add a word to finish the sentence. Help with spelling if needed.

My favorite toy is the ___.

Words to talk about

passenger	engine	tracks
roundhouse	mountain	valley

Words to read

what	said	was
four	that	green
but	gum	tug
cut	mug	rub

2

3

Name _____

 Write  Color

c t

b s

t b

Uu

p n

t p

n t

 Directions: Write *i*, *o*, or *u* to finish each word. Color the /u/ pictures.

 Home Activity: Have your child write *rug* and *bug* and draw a picture for each word.

Name _____

 **Write**  **Color**

what	am	said	was

_____
- -
I _____ five.

_____
- -
_____ can I do?

_____
- -
I _____ four.

_____
- -
I _____ I can help.

Directions: Write the missing word to finish each sentence. Color the pictures.

 Home Activity: Have your child use the high-frequency words in other sentences.

Jan and Gus are on the rug.

Jan and Gus are pals.

Jan and Gus

Jan and Gus are pals.

They like to have fun.

Jan and Gus like the sun.

They like to hum on the bus.

Jan and Gus see a bug.

They run in the mud.

Name _____

 Color

 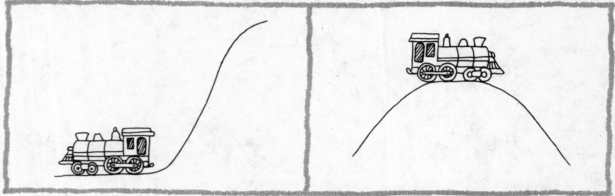

Directions: Color the picture that shows what would happen next in each story.

 Home Activity: Have your child tell what he or she does after putting on his or her pajamas.

Name _____

 Circle  Color

rag rug		cab cub	
hum ham		hut hat	

Directions: Circle the word that names the picture.
Color the /u/ pictures.

 Home Activity: Have your child draw a picture of something with /u/.

Name _____

✏️ **Draw**

 Directions: Draw a picture to show what would happen next in each story.

 Home Activity: With your child, retell a familiar story. You begin the story and ask your child to tell what happens next.

Name _____

 Color

| **People** | **Places** | **Things** |

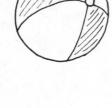

Directions: Color the picture of a person in the first box, a picture of a place in the second box, and a picture of a thing in the third box.

 School + Home

Home Activity: Point to pictures in a book. Ask your child to name each one and tell whether the picture shows a person, place, or thing.

Circle the pictures that begin with /v/. Color the pictures that begin with /z/.

Family Times

You are your child's first teacher!

This week we're ...

Reading *On the Move!*

Talking About Travel Around the World

Learning About Connect /v/ to *Vv* and /z/ to *Zz*
Main Idea

4

1

Here are ways to help your child practice skills while having fun!

Day 1 **Read Together**

Write *v* on one note card and *z* on another. Have your child show you the card with the letter that makes the beginning sound in these words: *vest, zig, zipper, vase, zebra,* and *video.*

Day 2 **Read Together**

Have your child read the Phonics Story *Val's Top.* Find words that begin with /v/ and /z/.

Day 3 **Connect /v/ to Vv and /z/ to Zz**

Have your child add the letters *v* or *z* to make a word.

_ig   __an   __est   __est

Day 4 **Nouns**

Tell your child that in a sentence, the noun names a person, place, or thing. Ask your child to say the noun in each sentence: *The bee buzzed. The vest is blue.*

Day 5 **Practice Handwriting**

Have your child write the following /v/ and /z/ words.

zip   van   zoo   vest

Words to talk about

travel	**kayak**	**llama**
dogsled	**submarine**	
double-decker bus		

Words to read

where	**come**	**what**
was	**said**	**yellow**
van	**zip**	**vest**
zap	**vet**	**zest**

Name _____

✏ Write   🖍 Color

_____
- - - - - - - - - - - - - - - - - - -
_____

_____
- - - - - - - - - - - - - - - - - - -
_____

_____
- - - - - - - - - - - - - - - - - - -
_____

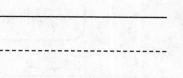

Vv
Zz

_____
- - - - - - - - - - - - - - - - - - -
_____

_____
- - - - - - - - - - - - - - - - - - -
_____

_____
- - - - - - - - - - - - - - - - - - -
_____

 Directions: Name each picture. Write *v* if the word begins with /v/. Write *z* if the word begins with /z/. Color the /v/ pictures.

 Home Activity: Have your child find other words that begin with /v/ or /z/.

Name _____

 Write  Color

| where | is | come | me |

_____

Do they see _____ ?

_____ here little dog.

_____ did you go?

My mom _____ here.

🍎 **Directions:** Write the missing word to finish each sentence. Color the pictures.

🏫 **School + Home** **Home Activity:** Have your child use the high-frequency words in other sentences.

© Pearson Education K

He will zap the tag.

Val has got the red top.

4

Val's Top

Val and Mom come in a van.

They will go to look for a top.

1

Val and Mom see a top.

They can zip it up.

The top is red.

Val and Mom like the top.

Name _____

 Color

Directions: Color the picture that illustrates the main idea of the story *On the Move!*

 Home Activity: With your child, retell a familiar story. Ask your child to tell the main idea of the story.

Name _____

 Write    Color

_____
ip

_____
et

_____
an

Vv
Zz

_____
est

_____
oo

_____
ero

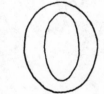

 Directions: Write *v* if the word begins with /v/. Write *z* if the word begins with /z/. Color the /z/ pictures.

School + Home **Home Activity:** Have your child draw pictures of things that begin with /v/ and /z/.

Name _____

 Color

 Directions: Draw a picture to show what
Messenger, Messenger is all about.

 Home Activity: Have your child tell about each
picture.

Practice Book Unit 5

Comprehension Main Idea **49**

Name _____

 Circle  Write

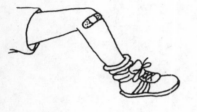

leg

run

_____

- - - - - - - - - - - - - - - - - - -

My _____ got cut.

sit

pal

_____

- - - - - - - - - - - - - - - - - - -

This is my _____.

pig

big

_____

- - - - - - - - - - - - - - - - - - -

Come here little _____.

hop

bug

_____

- - - - - - - - - - - - - - - - - - -

Look at the _____.

van

will

_____

- - - - - - - - - - - - - - - - - - -

That _____ is big.

hit

hill

_____

- - - - - - - - - - - - - - - - - - -

Run up the _____.

 Directions: Circle the noun that matches the picture. Write the word to complete the sentence.

 School + Home **Home Activity:** Have your child read each sentence.

Circle the pictures that begin with /y/. Color the pictures that begin with /kw/.

4

Family Times

You are your child's first teacher!

This week we're ...

Reading *This Is the Way We Go to School*

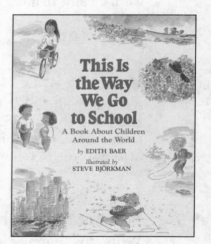

Talking About School Transportation

Learning About Connect /y/ to *Yy* and /kw/ to *Qq*
Draw Conclusions

1

Here are ways to help your child practice skills while having fun!

Day 1 | **Read Together**

Write these *q* and *y* words: *quit, quack, yes,* and *yam.* Read the words, pointing out the beginning sounds. Then help your child use the words in sentences.

Day 2 | **Read Together**

Have your child read the Phonics Story *Run, Tim.* Find words that have *y* and *q.*

Day 3 | **Connect /y/ to Yy and /kw/ to Qq**

Have your child make words by adding the letter *y* to the first two words and the letters *qu* to the last two words. Point to and say the words with your child.

_et   _am   _ _ilt   _ _ack

Day 4 | **Verbs**

Ask your child what he or she likes to do. Tell your child that these words are verbs. Give examples, such as *run, jump,* and *swim.* Ask your child to use action words to tell what he or she did at school today.

Day 5 | **Practice Handwriting**

Write this sentence on paper. Have your child use action words to complete it. Tell your child that action words tell what people or things do. Help your child spell out the words. Then have your child write the entire sentence.

I ___ and ___.

2

Words to talk about

cable car	trolley	skis
Metro line	vaporetto	
horse-and-buggy		

Words to read

where	come	what
was	said	two
quack	yam	yes
quit	quick	yet

3

Name _____

 Write Color

Yy
Qq

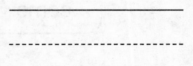

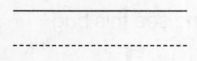 

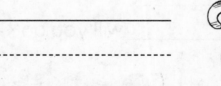

Directions: Name each picture. Write *y* if the word begins with /y/. Write *qu* if the word begins with /kw/. Color the /kw/ pictures.

Home Activity: Have your child find other words with /y/ or /kw/.

Phonics Consonants *Yy*/y/, *Qq*/kw/ **53**

Name _____

 Write    Color

| come   we   where   she |

_____

_____ can see me.

_____

_____ can run fast.

_____

_____ will you go?

_____

_____ and see this bug.

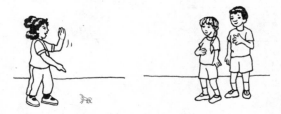

Directions: Write the missing word to finish each sentence. Color the pictures.

 Home Activity: Have your child use the high-frequency words in other sentences.

54 **High-Frequency Words**

Practice Book Unit 5

© Pearson Education K

Tim ran to the end.

Tim had a rest.

Phonics Story *Run Tim*
Target Skill Consonants *Yy/y/, Qq/kw/*

Run, Tim

Tim ran past his sis.

She said,

"You can not quit yet."

Tim ran up a hill.

His dad said,

"You can not quit yet."

Tim ran and ran.

His mom said,

"You can not quit yet."

Name _____

 Circle  Color

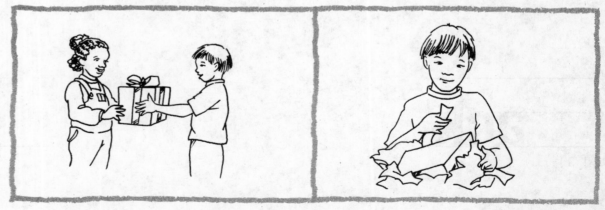

 Directions: Circle the picture that shows what you think the child would do next. Color the pictures.

 Home Activity: Have your child explain how they arrived at their conclusion.

Practice Book Unit 5

Comprehension Draw Conclusions **57**